Miracle Girl

Miracle Girl

Life Stories from a Xhosa Girl

Sivosethu Ndubela and Tony Pearce

MACMILLAN

First published in 2019 by
Pan Macmillan South Africa
Private Bag X19
Northlands
Johannesburg
2116

www.panmacmillan.co.za

ISBN 978-1-77010-671-0
e-ISBN 978-1-77010-672-7

*All of the photographs included have been supplied by the authors
from their personal collections.*

Editing by Katlego Tapala
Proofreading by Jane Bowman
Design and typesetting by Triple M Design, Johannesburg
Cover design by Zinelda McDonald
Front cover photograph by Liyema Ndubela
Back cover photograph by Thandokazi Jama

Printed and bound by **novus** *print*, a Novus Holdings company

To my family and friends for their love and support.
To the doctors and nurses who worked so hard to save
my life.
To the many people across the world who prayed for
my survival.
And to my God, who listened.

Acknowledgements

I would like to thank my guardians, Tony Pearce and his wife Lynn, for their support and encouragement in writing this book.

I would also like to thank my publisher, and my friends and family, who contributed and helped in any way that they could.

Contents

Foreword

My name is Tony Pearce. I live and work in the United Kingdom. In my business life I have a training school and qualified as a teacher in 2008. I decided to continue with my studies and achieved my BA (Hons) in Education. I was awarded a first-class degree so was given an award to continue and achieved a Masters degree in Education Research. I tell you this because it is how I came to have lived in South Africa for many months of each year and how I came to know Vovo.

For my dissertation I decided that I wanted to do unique work so I contacted my cousin Cornelia who lives in Port Elizabeth (P.E.) with an idea to research township education. My review of literature on this subject showed that there had been little or no studies completed on this subject. I was introduced to a charity called Zama which had contacts in New Brighton schools. I began a programme of teaching, observing and researching in two primary schools and one high school. I also committed a lot of time, four days every week to the Zama after-school project, teaching English using drama, music and dance as the vehicle of delivery. It was a successful formula and engaged the children and worked very well. At Zama, there was a wonderful Xhosa lady, Nkosi, who was much loved by all the children, and took me under her wing. I was like a fish out of water in those early days. Township life, isiXhosa culture and the all powerful 'community' was alien to me. I relied on Nkosi's help and support and we became good friends. I also taught her little daughters, first Vuvu and later Vovo. They worked very hard and impressed me with their talents; Vuvu as a singer and Vovo as a dancer.

In this story, you will read about the courage, strength, resilience and humour of a young Xhosa girl, Sivosethu Ndubela, whose nickname is Vovo. You will also read of some of the more negative aspects of life in South Africa's townships. As dramatic as some of these events might seem to you, unfortunately this is the reality for many young South Africans.

To introduce Vovo to you, I will tell you a short story not included in her narrative.

Once, Vovo was lying in her hospital bed, waiting for her early morning cup of tea. She was very sick and needed open-heart surgery. The nurses were short-staffed, and it was a busy night on the ward. Usually, at 4am they stopped for a cup of tea before waking all the patients, at 5am, to bath and have breakfast. The nurses usually made tea for themselves and for any patients that were already awake. But this night, they told

Vovo to make her own because they just did not have the time. Vovo got up, pushing her drip along on its stand, and went to the kitchen. She made tea for all of the nurses and any patients who wanted a drink, taking one cup at a time and delivering it.

The nurses told me of her kindness and when I asked her about it, she laughed and said, 'Don't worry Tony, it won't happen again. They all said that my tea is so disgusting, they will never drink it again!'

The Xhosa people have a culture of sharing. It is called ubuntu. This basically means, I am because you are. In other words, 'How can I enjoy my cup of tea, if you don't have one as well?' Vovo is a true example of ubuntu.

Tony Pearce
January 2019

Chapter 1

Naughty Girl

Hi! I am Vovo and I would like to tell you my story. Let me introduce myself. My full name is Sivosethu Ndubela and I was a millennium baby, born at Livingstone Hospital, Port Elizabeth in South Africa, on 9 January 2000.

I am a Xhosa girl. My mother's name is Nonkosazana Ndubela. In our language, Nonkosozana means princess. She was a princess to me; we called her Nkosi. My father, not so much. He was called Sisa. I do not remember much about him because he was not a major part of my life. He did not live with us and people say that he was a thug. He was murdered by a gang in 2010. I was only ten years old at the time and I am told that he was withdrawing money from an ATM when he was attacked and shot. He suffered ten bullet wounds, so I think that this gang really wanted to be sure that he was dead.

AmaXhosa are my people, but we also have clans, which are important to us. Our traditional culture says that we take our clan from our father, and my father's clan is Mthembu. Our ceremonies are performed according to the traditions of our clan.

Murder, sickness, poverty and crime are everyday events and a part of life in the townships of South Africa. I do not want to burden you with the long list of people we know who have been killed or died through sickness, but all of my friends and, I am certain everyone living in a township, has such stories to tell.

As I have told you, my father was shot. My grandfather, Kidwell Tsoko, was also robbed and stabbed to death in 2006.

My mother, Nkosi, raised my sister and I in our house in the Red Location of New Brighton, Port Elizabeth. New Brighton, in particular the Red Location, was at the forefront of the struggle against apartheid 20 years ago. We were lucky, we had a small house, part of what is called 'formal housing' in South Africa. Many in our community live in 'informal housing', but I would not call those houses at all; they are shacks made from whatever people could find to put a roof over their children's heads. The floors are usually bare dirt and there is often no water available; they share communal chemical toilets and standpipes for water. The dirt floors can turn muddy during a rainstorm which swallows up their few belongings. Our little house has two bedrooms and a living room with a kitchen area at the back. We have hot and cold water, electricity and an outside toilet, but no bathroom. We bath by pouring water into a large plastic or metal tub, which we call isitya. So I would love a home with a bathroom; what I would not give for a bathroom! A private bath would be a luxury.

My mother was kind and gentle, but she could be tough if

she needed to be. She was bringing up me and my sister Vuvu on her own, as best as she could. Vuvu is three years older than me and we have a special relationship, most of the time. Vuvu's full name is Vuyolwethu Ndubela. She is called Vuvu, which is why I am called Vovo. I think Vuvu and Vovo are easier to say than Vuyolwethu and Sivosethu, but I always wanted to be called Sethu, for short.

You could say that I am biased, but I believe that Vuvu is beautiful and a very talented singer. But back when we were younger she could be very naughty and so I had a good teacher. When Vuvu was about four years old, she would throw tantrums. To get her own way, she would scream and threaten to smash the windows with any weapon she could get her hands on. If Mum tried to pick her up, she would hold onto the handle of a broom, close to a window, shaking it. We could not afford new glass for the windows, so Mama was very careful, and grabbed Vuvu just in time. Many families beat their children harshly. Even in schools today, whether it's legal or not, teachers sometimes beat their students for 'respect'. My mother had her own way. She would pretend to forgive us. Come bath time, we would be naked, standing in the tub, waiting to be bathed, when out would come the wet dishcloth! She used to flick it on our bums, and it would hurt! She was a great marksman with that dishcloth and she hardly ever missed. It left red marks on our buttocks, but this was better than what happened to some of our friends, who were often battered and bruised by their families.

In November 2002, my mother gave birth to a third little girl, but I don't remember much about it as I was just three years of age; my little sister died in February 2003, aged just three months.

I was four years old when my mother found work as a nurse in a Johannesburg hospital. Johannesburg is over 1 000 km from Port Elizabeth, so as happens in many South African families, my sister and I were sent to live with our grandmother, my mother's mother, so that Mama could leave for work.

Chapter 2

Cookhouse

My grandmother, Lulama Tsoko, lived in Cookhouse, which is a village of about 5 000 people, 170 km north of my home city, Port Elizabeth. It is still in the Eastern Cape Province, but slightly different. The main languages in Port Elizabeth are English and isiXhosa, whereas in Cookhouse it is Afrikaans and isiXhosa.

My grandmother, who we call Gogo, meaning granny, was a powerful sangoma. A sangoma is a traditional healer. There are good sangomas, and bad sangomas who cast spells and curse people. My Gogo was a good sangoma who used herbs, other traditional medicine and ritual ceremonies to cure people. She saved many lives.

Apart from Gogo and Vuvu, I also lived with my aunt and uncle in a huge house. It had a garage and a separate room outside, what we call emrhalweni, for all of my grandmother's traditional medicine, equipment and consultations.

Outside there were beehives, dogs and chickens. I used to chase the chickens and wring their necks when I was very young. I was once caught with my hands around the neck of a near dead chicken and Gogo beat me; Gogo was never harsh, so it was not so bad. I don't think that I was a cruel four-year-old, I had seen Gogo do the same before cooking them, so I was just copying her.

Gogo also sold meat in portions, as well as chocolates and bompies from the house. A bompie is juice frozen in a plastic sandwich bag, to make something like an ice lolly. My sister and I used to steal a little chocolate and tell Gogo that the rats ate it; there are rats living in, under or next to every township home. Then I would open the bompies and suck all of the colour and flavour out of them, leaving just white ice. Her customers came back shouting at her holding up little plastic bags of ice water. She would be so embarrassed, and when they left she came straight to my room, putting her hands tightly around my neck to punish me. It sounds worse than it felt, I promise.

Despite my naughtiness, Gogo always spoiled me and Vuvu. She loved us, and we loved and respected her. One day, three of Gogo's friends arrived and they sat around gossiping while my sister served them little snacks. It was a hot day and they were very thirsty so they asked me for water. I was surprised and puzzled because I was very small – I could not reach the top of the sink and so I certainly couldn't reach the tap and turn it on. I did not want to say anything because we had to respect our elders. I went to the kitchen and found a jug and a small cup. Then I went to the toilet and took water out of the toilet bowl with the cup and put it in the jug. I took it to the ladies, who drank every drop, and even asked for more! But then there was a problem —I had given them all of the water from the toilet bowl and I was far too short to flush the toilet to refill it. So I was leaning into the toilet with my legs sticking out, trying to find the remnants of water at the bottom, when my uncle heard me and came to find out what I was doing. I told him and he fell over laughing. He told Gogo and her guests. They were gagging and wanted to vomit but all my uncle could do was laugh. I did not get punished though; they realised that it wasn't my fault that I was too young and too short.

One day my mother came to visit us at our grandmother's house in Cookhouse and we all sat in the living room. My father, Sisa, had given me a very lifelike, evil looking, remote-controlled snake. I hid with the remote control and I sent the snake hissing and slithering into the living room. It looked so real that even Mama, Gogo and my aunt, Babalwa, jumped up screaming. My mother ran out of the house to our neighbours, so fast that even those neighbours were frightened. Aunt Babalwa also ran but tripped and fell, knocking herself unconscious. After about an hour, my uncle and Gogo came back and went to our neighbours' house to get my mother. Aunt Babalwa was still asleep on the floor. Everyone was terrified. So I held up the toy snake and remote and I admitted to what I had done, but I could not stop laughing. I was sent to Gogo's bedroom and locked in. But still, every time I thought about the screaming and the looks on their faces, I rolled about laughing.

After what seemed like hours in that room I got bored, so I climbed out of the window. I stole fruit from my grandmother's fruit trees and sold it, going from door to door. I made good money and when I had sold everything I returned home. But I had forgotten that I had climbed out the window and so I went back in through the front door. Big mistake! Huge mistake! My mother grabbed me and asked, 'How did you get out of that room?' She hit me, but I did not mind as I had been on a great adventure and had a lot of fun. To this day, I laugh about that snake.

Sometimes the whole family would gather at Gogo's house – the Tsokos and the Ndubelas – which was so much fun and a great opportunity to be naughty and play pranks on them. I had a little cousin, Siseko Tsoko, who loved dressing up. He would make me laugh, putting on my sister's dresses and heels, then parading around the room. He caused a lot of trouble, cutting up my mother's wigs to put on his head. We were thrown out of the house and into the garden to play, so we pooed on Gogo's vegetables. My uncle caught us in the act. He did not hit us, worse, he cut off all our hair. As God is my judge, I hated that man at that moment. He shaved our heads. I was only five years old, but I refused to attend church. I did not want to go to school either but my mother made me go. All the other kids were laughing at me. They said that I had a head like an ostrich egg. I was so angry and upset that I did not want to go back to school. My grandma went to see the principal the following day and all the teasing and jokes stopped.

As I mentioned earlier, my grandmother was a highly respected sangoma. On one occasion my aunt and uncle, who helped to look after us, had gone to Port Elizabeth so Vuvu and I were left with Gogo. She was asked to perform a traditional ceremony in Fort Beaufort. Fort Beaufort is a small town approximately 90 km from our home in Cookhouse. Vuvu and I were so excited. We were too young to be left home alone so Gogo took us with her. I was very proud of her as she treated people with traditional herbs and healed them. Gogo was so impressive; she had such passion for her calling. She did this to help people, not just for the money. She performed the ceremony and was given two goats and a cow. The cow was slaughtered and cooked at Fort Beaufort and shared with the people. However, as usual, I saw this as a great opportunity to play pranks. In the bushveld area near Fort Beaufort, next to where the traditional ceremony was held, there are spiders. In South Africa, we have huge spiders. Sometimes they are hairy and bigger than a man's hand. The ones I caught in a box might not have been the biggest, but they were still a bit scary. I put them in the bedrooms and on the beds of the people attending the ceremony. If you have never seen a Xhosa person turn white, there is no better way than letting them find a big spider in bed with them. I think that they suspected that I was the villain, but no one could prove it, so I was relieved to get away with that trick.

I used to watch my uncle fix things. He was the mechanic

in our house and fixed the kettle or iron when it broke. I wanted to be a mechanic like him. I decided to mend the plug socket and stuck my finger in it. Of course I got a shock. Then I tried to fix our iron, while it was plugged in. I got another electrical shock. I was too young to understand, but I did not let that stop me. I took Gogo's radio apart; when she walked in I was sat on the floor surrounded by bits of her radio. She said that she was tired of smacking me and just sent me outside. So I stole 50 cents to buy some bubblegum. I chewed it for a while, then put it on Gogo's ceremonial sangoma clothes and then I went back out to play. She knew immediately who the culprit was. She grabbed me and started to strangle me. She forgot that she was tired of punishing me. I shouted for my mother to help me. She said, 'Your mother is not here, just me!' I looked at her and I felt an urge to laugh, but instead, I pretended I was fainting. I went quiet and limp, like I was passing out. Gogo got so worried, crying out, 'Xolo! Xolo!' which means 'Sorry! Sorry!' I so loved my grandmother, and after all the commotion I said, 'No Gogo, you have nothing to be sorry for, I was wrong'.

In 2005, Vuvu and I were enrolled in a local school called Visrivier, which is Afrikaans for Fish River. I attended Grade R, the reception class, and my sister went into Grade 3. I am sure that we were good students because I passed and was promoted to Grade 1 and Vuvu to Grade 4. Gogo was pleased and proud.

She cooked us a very special and delicious meal that night.

At the end of that academic year, in December 2006, my mother arrived to fetch us and take us back with her to live in our little home in P.E. I would be turning seven years old the following January. Vuvu, an August baby, was aged ten. We loved Gogo, so it was a sad time, but we also loved our mum, so it was exciting for us to move back in with her.

Chapter 3

Friends

The two years in Cookhouse at Gogo's house seemed like forever to me as a tiny six-year-old. We had left behind our home, most of our family, friends and school. I was definitely excited to be going with my mum, who I adored, back to Port Elizabeth, but at the same time I was sad.

At first I hated it back in P.E. I had no friends and friends are very important to me. I love my friends and I like to think that I am loyal and caring. My family and friends help me to deal with all of the challenges and problems I face in my life. Without them I do not do too well and I get sad if I am alone.

The first friend I made when I returned to Port Elizabeth was Zikhona Ngayeka, who lived next door. Zikhona was also a naughty girl, just like me. In fact, her nickname is Nomqoki, which means exactly that – Naughty Girl! Zikhona is nearer Vuvu's age so we became a gang of three. We did the usual things, like knock and run. We would go to apartments close by, knock on people's doors and then run away before they could answer. We also skipped and played hide and seek like the other, more well-behaved kids. Our little group grew, with

Thandile, Athi, Simnikiwe and Sinethemba joining us to play.

Sometimes we would go behind a shop close to our house. We would take tins from home, like empty bean tins or fruit tins. We would all steal a little food from home – a stock cube, rice, mince, a potato, whatever we could find. Then we would build a fire and cook the food in the tins on our little fire. One day, we needed more wood for our fire, so a boy said that he would watch our food while we hunted for twigs. When we came back, all our food was gone. I was so angry –why would anybody play such a prank?!

We learned to cook at home. Vuvu and I love to cook so it was not difficult for us and Mama was a kind and patient teacher. We washed dishes, cleaned our room and were taught how to wash and iron clothes. We learnt all the chores that most Xhosa children do to help at home.

It was not always easy to cook at home. Sometimes there was very little food, or no money for food, especially near the end of the month. We managed to cook delicious food with whatever fresh meat we could, thanks to our mother teaching us so well. We tried to use a lot of vegetables, soups and rice, but sometimes there was only mealie-meal, flour, or samp and beans to eat. We also ate chicken heads, chicken feet or necks if we could not afford any other meat.

In Port Elizabeth, Vuvu and I were enrolled in Abraham Levy Primary School. This is a city school, not a township school, so we had to take a school bus or a minibus taxi. We attended

Abraham Levy because my mother wanted us to learn English and continue learning Afrikaans. Because of this, my sister and I are a little unusual in our township. In school, our primary language is English and our second language is Afrikaans, but at home we speak isiXhosa, the native language of my people the amaXhosa. So we are trilingual. We say Xhosa for short for both our people and our language.

Obviously, it is safer to be closer to home and attend school nearby, but because of the deliberately unequal way in which the education of black people was approached by the government under apartheid, some township schools do not always offer good education. My mother felt it was worth the financial sacrifice to send us into the city to be educated. But my sister and I have been robbed of our taxi fare, even lunch and earrings sometimes, as have many of our friends, as we walked to school from the bus stop or taxi rank.

At first, I hated everything about Abraham Levy Primary School. We had come from a countryside school in Cookhouse to a large city school. It was 6 km from home, in a big, noisy city and I was only six years old. I went to school with Vuvu, but sometimes we could not travel home together. Vuvu made friends very quickly so I felt quite lonely and frightened, with a lot of strangers around me in the taxi, if she wasn't there.

I think that there were 34 children in my class, 1B. This is another advantage of city schools because in my local school in New Brighton, there were more than 50 children in a small

14

classroom and it was difficult to learn in that environment.

I soon made friends though, and my first good friends were Zolisiwe and Asemahle, but our group grew and grew. Every class was different, and our class suited me well. It was noisy, full of energy and a lot of laughter. One day, my friend and I stole our teacher's lunch from off her desk. We then wrote her a note and left it on her desk:

'Dear Teacher, thank you for the lunch, it was delicious'
We did not sign it.

We were all great friends up until Grade 6. Then there was a lot of teasing. Not friendly teasing, but hurtful insults and gossiping about each other. I had a physical fight with a boy in our group, we really beat each other up. Our friends split us up and called the teacher, who hit us on the hand with a piece of plastic pipe. He asked us what the problem was and I could not answer him; I was too angry to even talk. I think the teacher saw that there was a problem with the whole class, not just the two of us who were fighting, so he punished the whole class, using the pipe. That boy and I became firm enemies for about a week, and then we started to get along again.

I must now tell you about one of my most embarrassing moments. I don't want to tell you, but it is true, and it is part of my story. I was in Grade 4, so I was nine years old. The previous evening, at home, had been tough. Firstly, I was playing outside the house when I saw a snake. It scared me, so I screamed. My mother came out, grabbed me, threw a stone at its head to scare it away, and took me inside the house. After an hour, I went back outside to play. I have no idea what the game was, but it involved me putting my leg down a drain. I screamed for help and my uncle tried to pull me out, but I was stuck. The neighbours tried to help, my mother tried; no one could get me out. I don't cry when things like this happen. I get angry. I was so angry. My leg had been stuck down the drain for around two hours! My uncle's friend arrived and decided to help. My uncle and his friend pulled so hard that I screamed with the pain, but they got me out. Finally! My mother bathed me, gave me food and got me ready for bed.

But the day was not over. I felt something irritating inside my ear. I got a cotton bud – how could this go wrong? It snapped, deep inside my ear! I could not get it out and began to panic. I tried tweezers and a needle, but had no luck. I went to my mother, crying, to show her what I had done. She asked, 'Why are you like this, Vovo? Why is it always you?' She tried to get it out but failed. My uncle and his friend also tried. It took an hour to get that cotton bud out. I looked at myself in the mirror and asked myself, 'Why am I always in trouble?' At that moment, I prayed to change the way I am, but of course I never changed. I was still the same.

The following day I went to school, but I was not feeling well. I always went to school, no matter what, because I missed my school friends. I was bored without them. I was on the bus when my stomach started aching and grumbling. This was bad. I had the most terrible wind that you can imagine. People started opening windows. The passengers began arguing about whether the toxic smell was coming from the inside or the outside of the bus. Then suddenly, the wind got really bad. I soiled myself. The smell got worse; I opened my window and complained to distract any attention from myself. The passengers were complaining to the driver that someone or something had died on his bus! My friend Zolisiwe asked me what was wrong. I said, 'Nothing, I am just tired.'

I took off my jersey and tied it round my waist to hide my dirty skirt. Zolisiwe did not believe I was tired. She asked me again what was wrong. I told her the truth, that I had a runny tummy and that I had made a real mess of myself. She just laughed and went with me to the toilets. We cleaned my skirt and washed my panties. I put my skirt back on but left my underwear off. Zolisiwe called a teacher to help me; I was so embarrassed my cheeks felt like they were burning. The teacher found me a school tracksuit to wear and called my mother to take me home.

Chapter 4

Zama

There was an old abandoned school near our home, called Arthur Nyobo, where we used to play sometimes. In 2009, a project was set up to help children in our area. It was called the Zama Project and they used some of the better looking class-rooms of the school for this. 'Zama' means 'Try' and my mother found work with them as a teacher. It was an after-school project that taught children lots of skills like knitting, playing chess, sewing, games, and classes in reading and English. My sister and I loved to attend whenever we could. There was a modelling competition and my sister won Miss Zama for mod-elling dresses. I modelled jeans and won Miss Jeans.

On 8 January 2010, my mother gave birth to my little sis-ter, Iviwe. She had to give up working at Zama for a while to care for Iviwe. Vuvu and I were very happy. My mother looked after us and our new sister. As we got older I became a little less naughty and clumsy. My beloved grandmother retired from being a sangoma. She sold her large house in Cookhouse and moved to a little house in Kwazakhele that had been owned by my grandfather and was passed on to her after his death. Having Gogo close by again completed our little family.

Around this time, we met a guy from the United Kingdom who worked as a volunteer for Zama. His name is Tony Pearce and he taught us drama and music. We put on shows locally and built ourselves up to perform at the Savoy Theatre in the city centre. The audience loved our show and they were singing and dancing in the aisles. The show was recorded and a DVD was made. I performed traditional dances with other children and my talented sister sang Whitney Houston's *I Will Always Love You*. So that you can meet her and hear her sing, there are YouTube links at the end of my story, where you can also see me.

Not only was Tony important because he helped us to learn drama and perform shows, he holds a special significance in my life to this day. He worked at Zama with my mother and they became good friends. Tony regularly returned to the UK, where he ran his businesses, but he came back often, sometimes with his wife, Lynn. She is kind and funny and she is also an important person in my life.

Zama was going to close, but Tony started a new organisation called Location Kids, which is a not-for-profit organisation (NPO). It kept all our friends together and we performed in a lot of shows including at the amphitheatre at the Victoria and Alfred (V&A) Waterfront in Cape Town. This was a lot of fun and everything in my life seemed good. Townships can be tough, but we had a happy family and we were doing well at school. Location Kids kept us busy with one project after another. I did not know it then, but everything was soon to change.

Chapter 5

Nkosi

In 2011, when I was eleven years old, my mother started to get sick. She had severe arthritis in her hands, legs and feet. The pain was crippling her. It was worse in the winter time, especially when it was cold and wet. The pain was not bad all the time and sometimes she seemed to be fine. However, over time the arthritis got worse and worse. She had to give up work. I knew a little of how she was feeling because I also started to get arthritic pains in my legs and ankles. Later, it was also in my arms.

Mama was really struggling with the pain and life became so tough. We had no money and very little food. We could not buy medicine for her and the clinic only gave us Panado. Sometimes Tony bought Nurofen for her which helped a lot, at least for a little while. My mother was sad about what was happening to our family, and I hated to see how upset she became. I did not want to add to her problems. I forced my school shoes onto my swollen feet and forced myself to walk so that my pain would not make her feel worse and add to her pain. My legs and feet hurt so much it made my eyes wet with tears. My little sister was only a year old, and my mother was in too much pain to even lift her sometimes.

At home, the house was becoming a ruin. There was no money for food, let alone repairs. The roof leaked and the wooden floor in the kitchen area collapsed as it was rotten. The rats ripped through our furniture to make nests. If the rats were looking for food in our house they would starve to death. Our clothes smelled mouldy. Our friends started to notice, but Vuvu and I told everyone that everything was okay. We are a proud family. The poor state of the house and little food probably helped to give our already sick Mama tuberculosis (TB).

Tony arrived at Port Elizabeth Airport just after New Year 2013. He had arranged for us to meet him and his cousin Cornelia, who also lives in P.E. and she gave us a lift to the Willows, where Tony stays when he is in South Africa. I could see in Tony's eyes, as soon as he saw us, that he knew something was wrong. Maybe it was the smell or our tummies rumbling, but he knew. He asked us, but Vuvu and I told him that everything was fine. I was so pleased to see him, and I hoped that he would make everything fine again.

Tony went to see our mother, who asked him if he would look after us while she was unwell. 'Of course,' he agreed. He collected our clothes and took us to live with him at Willow Grove in Summerstrand. Willow Grove is a site by the Indian Ocean, safe and secure, where we stayed in a three-bedroom cottage. It was clean and fresh. Tony made us a meal and washed our clothes. We started to feel so much better. Mama only had to look after Iviwe and my aunt helped her.

My mother seemed so much better; she came with Iviwe to Willow Grove to visit us, and we all went out for a meal together. Mama said that we smelled beautiful and hugged us. For the first time in nearly a year, I felt very happy. It was not going to last.

My mother was back in hospital on my thirteenth birthday, and I was determined not to celebrate. Mama was so sick and I think she knew it. It was then that she asked Tony, for the first time, if he would become our guardian if she became too sick to care for us. He said that if Mama wanted that and Vuvu and I agreed – as well as our family – then of course he would care for us.

On 21 January 2013, Mama sent a message asking to see Tony alone, without us. He went to the house in Kwazakhele to see her. He later told us that she was very thin; lying on a mattress in the living room and looking very sick. Mama asked Tony, in front of my family, to care for me and my sister if she died and she asked the family to honour her wish for her children.

That night, Mama was admitted to Dora Nginza Hospital in Port Elizabeth. Tony did tell us that Mama was in hospital, but we stuck to our routine. Vuvu went to her high school, David Livingstone, and I was still at Abraham Levy, close by. We had planned to visit Mama at 3pm during the visiting hours, so it was strange to see Tony arrive at my school, with Vuvu, at 10:15am. He arranged for me to leave school and I got into the car. Tony told us that he thought we should go to the hospital right away. We were in the car when my aunt called Tony on his cellphone (mobile) to say that my mother had died.

It was the worst minute, of the worst hour, of the worst day of my life. The pain I felt was so bad, I screamed and cried. I could not stop crying. Vuvu and I held each other, tears pouring down our faces. Only someone who has lost their special, loving mother can know that pain.

Tony took us to the house in Kwazakhele where our family was gathered in shock and sadness. Nkosi, Mama, was dead and she was only 38 years old. I was an orphan at just thirteen years old.

Chapter 6

The Funeral

Sadness does not begin to describe how I felt. Sad is when an apple is mouldy inside or when you get a low mark in a subject at school. I am not that great with words in English, but I think 'anguish' is what I felt, and my sense of loss has never gone away. I think of Mama every single day of my life.

Tony took over the role of being our guardian straight away. He talked to our family about dates for the funeral. He had to go to Cape Town to meet his wife, Lynn, who was flying in from the UK with their grandson, Ethan. Tony decided to take us with him, to shelter us from the sadness of the funeral preparations.

Vuvu and I took a flight for the first time in our lives. It was amazing! We were in Cape Town, 750 kilometres away, within an hour. We checked in at the Harbour Edge Apartments, which are very beautiful. The view from the back balcony is of Table Mountain. The front balcony looks over the famous Victoria and Alfred Waterfront.

That evening, I had my first experience of what it was like to belong in a white family. We sat with Tony and talked about our future. Tony asked our opinions and discussed everything with us. In many black families, it is common to just tell children what to do, to tell them nothing about the problems the family is facing and never really discuss anything with them. It is good in some ways not to be involved in adult problems, but Tony told us that he would listen to our ideas and wishes and take them into consideration, before making the final decision. He even asked us if we *wanted* him and Lynn to be our guardians; no matter what he and Mama had agreed on, this arrangement would never work, he said, if we didn't want it that way. Of course, it was a 'no-brainer'. It felt good to talk about our future, our education, where we would live and how this would work, especially what would happen when Tony returned to the UK.

The next day we arrived at Cape Town International Airport to pick up Lynn and Ethan. Lynn gave us lots of hugs and cuddles and told us how upset she was that Mama had passed away. Ethan was a little shy; he is only one year older than me.

While we were in Cape Town, we went up Table Mountain in the cable car and even had lunch up there. The views were amazing. We went shopping around the V&A and took a boat ride out into the bay. I was still hurting inside but did not feel quite as lonely and hopeless. Back at the hotel we all went swimming in the pool. Ethan was less shy now, but he was always polite and well-mannered – very different to the experience I had with other boys I had grown up around.

Our time in Cape Town was over too soon; we flew back to Port Elizabeth and back to reality. We had not been allowed to see our mother in the hospital mortuary because we were under 18, but a little prayer meeting was arranged at the funeral home and we got to see Mama in her coffin. She was at peace. I was not at peace, that deep feeling of anguish came back to me. I often felt that I wanted to die as well, but I looked at my sisters, and I knew that we had to be there for each other. It was what our mother would want for us. Iviwe was too young to understand fully, but she was very sad.

All the arrangements were made for the funeral and a date was set for 2 February 2013. Lynn took us shopping for suitable clothes and shoes to wear. Xhosa funerals can be quite long. There is a prayer vigil the night before. We were staying at Willow Grove with Tony and Lynn, so the next day we had to drive for over an hour to Kwazakhele to make it there by 7am. It was a very hot Saturday. When we got there many people had already arrived, and my sister and I had to greet them all. My friends from Location Kids had come to sing at the funeral. My mother was brought from the funeral home to the house, where we prayed. Again, we were able to see Mama and say goodbye. I never want to feel the same kind of pain inside again. It was really bad.

At the service, some of Mama's friends gave short speeches. I, too, said a few words to tell her that I loved her. Vuvu was crying so much that she could not say her speech, so Tony read it for her. In it, she promised Mama that she would do her best to be a mother to Iviwe and me. Tony also said a few words, promising our mother that he would honour his commitments for as long as we needed him.

After the service there was another ceremony near the graveside. We had prayers and songs. As our mother's coffin was lowered into her grave, we put flowers on top. I broke down and cried again.

As we walked back to the road from the grave, we saw a big coach run over a woman. Its huge double wheels crushed and killed her. That lady is buried next to Mama in Motherwell Cemetery. It is strange, I was already too numb to actually be shocked by her badly crushed and bloodied body.

After the funeral, we returned to the house in Kwazakhele with the other mourners, for lunch. There was a family meeting and our uncles asked to see Tony and Lynn. My great-uncle told them that they would respect Mama's dying wish for them to be our guardians. It was also agreed that we would live with our grandmother, aunt and uncle in the house in Kwazakhele, because our house in New Brighton was not fit to live in. When Tony and Lynn visited Port Elizabeth, we would live with them at Willow Grove.

Chapter 7

Sammy

Once the funeral ceremonies were over, Tony took me to the doctor to find out about my arthritis. I was given painkillers, anti-inflammatory tablets and gels to rub onto sore parts. This took a lot of the pain away. For a while.

Tony and Lynn returned to England and we went back to school. At Abraham Levy Primary School, the teachers and my friends asked me what had happened and why I had missed school. They were shocked to hear the news that my mother had died. There was a competition for electing a 'school hero'. I thought that a very popular, pretty and intelligent girl would win the vote, but I was wrong. I was elected 'hero'. I was so proud! I gave a little speech and thanked everyone. Even the popular girl who lost clapped and said, 'Well done Vovo, you deserve it!'

My sister's school, David Livingstone, was failing her, with the teachers on strike and very poor results. Often, the school was closed. Tony moved her to Morningside High School; this was a better school, in a nicer part of the city. Tony had to pay the fees, but at the time David Livingstone was in such a bad state, this was the only way Vuvu could have a chance at an education.

I passed my Grade 7 exams, so I too was placed in Morningside High School. Our farewell party at Abraham Levy was wonderful. I was all dressed up and my family said that I looked beautiful, just like my mother. Tony arranged for me to go with a friend. He also arranged a surprise: a huge, white limousine arrived to take us to the dance! We even had alcohol-free champagne to sip on as we were driven to school. It was a magical night.

Morningside was not that great. I was lonely. I did see Vuvu, but she had her own friends. I did not know anyone, and I felt so alone, again. I was placed into 8C, a funny and naughty class, but with good, clever students. I soon found my first friend and we chatted and spent break times together. Soon out little band grew. I missed all of my friends from Abraham Levy who now went to different schools, but it was getting easier.

Just after my mother's funeral, when Tony had returned to the UK, Vuvu fell pregnant. She was only sixteen years old. I can only think that she was desperately unhappy and looking for someone to love her. The problem was that she never told anyone. I believe that she would not even admit it to herself. There is nothing new in teenagers falling pregnant, but we did not know what Tony would say; would he give up on us now?

Tony was so angry. He had noticed how big Vuvu was becoming and asked her whether she was pregnant. He even made her take a pregnancy test which somehow produced a negative result. She lied to him, the one thing he hates. He always says we can deal with anything if we know the truth. He was more upset about the lies than the pregnancy. When my aunt took Vuvu to the clinic, she was already seven months pregnant. There was no other choice, she had to have the baby.

We need not have worried about Tony. He may have wanted to strangle Vuvu, but he flew over to be with her at the hospital for the birth of my niece, Sammy, on 27 November 2013.

Samantha Nkosi Ndubela, named after our mother, is a beautiful and intelligent girl with a very dry sense of humour. Obviously I think that Sammy is very special, but I will tell you a couple of stories so that you can judge for yourself. One day she was in the back of Tony's car, sitting on Vuvu's knee. She was about fifteen months old at the time. Vuvu was struggling to get out of the car while carrying Sammy. Sammy turned to her mother, looked at her seriously with her big eyes and said, 'If you drop me, I will make you pay!'

When she was three years old, Tony was singing as we drove on a long journey. Sammy said, 'Tony! Singing is not for you.' Then she turned the radio up to its highest volume and told her mother, 'I would rather listen to that.' Sammy's quotes are now legendary.

But we had nearly lost her too. Vuvu, Sammy and I were staying at Willow Grove with Tony, Lynn and our friend Gemma, who is also from the UK and volunteers to teach modern dancing to the children at Location Kids. At about six months old, Sammy had a chest infection and Tony sat up with her all night, but she was getting worse. She was just a baby. We went to school as usual and Tony and Lynn took Sammy to a private clinic. The nurses at the clinic sent them to the doctor's surgery next door. Dr Smith checked her quickly, wrote a note and sent them immediately to the paediatric department at the public hospital, Dora Nginza, where my mother had died. Dr Smith had asked Tony to keep him informed of Sammy's progress. At Dora, Tony pushed his way to the front of a long queue and put the note in the doctor's hand. Sammy was immediately examined and put on a nebuliser. She was very ill; she had bronchitis and influenza at the same time, and was also developing pneumonia. I was so upset. I could not bear to lose my niece. It was so unfair, I had just lost my mother. Sammy was admitted to the children's ward.

After a couple of days, Sammy started to get better. Tony phoned the surgery to tell the doctor the good news. The doctor said, 'She is a very lucky child. She was very close to respiratory failure and I expected you to call and tell me that she had died.'

Some of my family members wanted Vuvu to leave school to look after Sammy, and to wash laundry, cook and clean at home. This was the first argument between Tony and some of my family members. He said that Vuvu's life was not over because of Sammy; she should continue going to school. They all got very angry, but my grandmother said that we, as a family, had agreed that Tony would be our guardian and it didn't matter who liked, or did not like his decision, as it was his choice to make. Vuvu remained at Morningside.

She was, however, getting very depressed. She obviously felt the loss of our mother very deeply and she also had depression after Sammy was born; she was arguing with friends at school and she was not doing well with her schoolwork. She was overtired; caring for Sammy, studying and doing chores at home. One evening, everything got too much for her and she wanted to be with Mama so she swallowed rat poison. She later told me that she felt her whole life was miserable and that she was letting everyone down.

She was admitted to Livingstone Hospital where they thought that she might die. Tony flew over from England, and fortunately Vuvu pulled through. He took her and Sammy away to talk everything over with her. I am not sure what they talked about, but she seemed happier when she came home. Tony and Lynn agreed to pay for a créche for Sammy, to ease the pressure on Vuvu.

Sammy loved attending crèche. One day she came home and said that she had passed to the next class. So every time she was asked to do something, like pick up her toys, she would say, 'I don't have to do that – I passed!'

Chapter 8

Xhosa Culture

I cannot tell you more of my story without explaining a little bit of our culture. I am unusual because I was born and raised as a Xhosa girl, but for the last five years, since I was thirteen years old, I have had a white guardian from a different country and culture. Whilst this is unusual, I am also lucky.

Tony always tells me to respect my culture and to never forget where I come from. It is unlikely that this would happen, but he tells me this and then argues with me about a lot of things that to me are very normal and true, but his culture tells him differently.

I am a Christian but like most Xhosa people, I talk to my ancestors. Many of our traditional ceremonies are centred around our ancestors and are about communicating with them. For example, imbeleko is a ceremony for boys and girls, where they are introduced to their ancestors. Imbeleko is compulsory in my culture, to ward off any bad luck we may have. Lynn cringes when I tell her that we kill a goat as part of the ceremony. Our home is stripped bare and we sleep in the living room with the dead goat. The offal is eaten first and then the meat is cooked and eaten in a specific order to ensure that the right people get the correct portion of meat. The horns of any animal that has been ceremonially slaughtered are nailed to a sacred pole in the garden. Historically, our people lived in roundhouses with no fridge. The soft tissue of the animal would quickly rot in the African heat if not eaten. They also had to bring the carcass indoors or the lions and wild dogs would carry away and eat our meat. There were no slaughterhouses or refrigerators in those times, and so the ceremonies we carry out today reflect our culture and history. The ceremony of imbeleko, within different clans, has slightly different procedures.

It is important to introduce ourselves to our ancestors and it is compulsory that we also do what they ask us of us. One day, Aunt Babalwa dreamt that her grandmother asked her for a meal. This meant that we, as a family, must buy a goat or a sheep to show our respect and cook the meal for our ancestors. Shortly after this, my uncle dreamt that his uncle was thirsty. So we had to make umqombothi, made from mealie-meal and sorghum malt and fermented with yeast. Once it has been made it is poured at the sacred pole in the garden, under the animal horns, as we talk to our ancestors.

The boys go to the mountains, where they are circumcised and taught lessons about the correct behaviour of men. A big ceremony and party are held on their return.

Before a Xhosa girl marries, her family would expect amalobolo, like a dowry, from the groom and his family. In the past this was in the form of a selection of livestock, but today it is often money that is given instead. This is because not as many of our people actually own livestock any more, so it is just easier to give money instead. Tony says that this is wrong, and he would never sell us like a piece of meat. But in our culture amalobolo – whether it is in the form of livestock or money – is a sign of respect and shows that the girl is worth so much to the groom that he is willing to give something to marry her. It is a way for the boy's family to show his intentions and to also show appreciation to the girl's family for raising her for them, as she will now be their daughter too. It is rare these days, but some girls have marriages that are arranged by their families, where they are given to older men, often as second or third wives. This happened to one of my friends and it really upset me. Tony says that this will never happen to us.

A recurring argument with Tony is, as you will see, I believe in ghosts and witches. Most of us do. Tony laughs at us and warns that superstition can hold us back. I believe in the powers of sangomas. Tony argues that much of it is false and it is only fear and belief that make it seem true. I always tell him that he does not understand. We believe that if you dream about a snake, for example, there is an enemy of the family who hates us. One night my sister had a dream about a snake in the house. She then dreamt that my mother killed that snake for us. We believe that this means our mother is protecting us even though she is not here; she is with us in spirit.

My grandmother used to see ghosts or hear footsteps in the house. If she knew no physical person was in the house, she would throw sea salt around the house and in her bed to protect herself. She would then light a herb called impepho that has been known to help many families, including our own, in getting rid of ghosts. Impepho is mostly used to open up communication with our ancestors, but it also has other uses, like the one I just mentioned. But after my grandmother died, we have only used salt.

There are other beliefs that Tony calls superstitions. If you see an owl, this means bad luck. If an owl comes into your house, this means someone will die in your house. If a bee comes into your home, this can mean your ancestors are with you or you are about to have a visitor. These are all facts to us.

It is okay that Tony does not understand what we believe, our cultures are different and we learn from each other. Some people in the Xhosa community believe differently too. There are compulsory ceremonies, like imbeleko and the boys going to the mountain to return as men, as I already mentioned, but a lot of the ceremonies are dictated by which church you belong to. Some churches don't uphold our culture, so families who belong to those churches don't perform these traditional ceremonies. But in my family we are known as traditionalists and we believe and follow those traditions.

I enjoy discussing these cultural differences with Tony. He told me about his culture, and I find it ... strange and exciting.

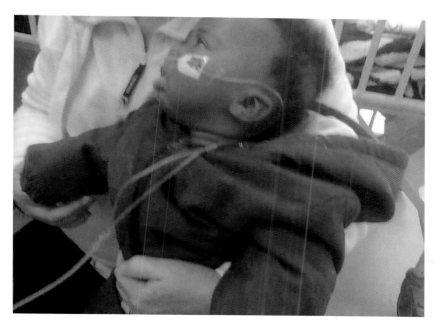

Above: My niece, Samantha (Sammy), when she was admitted to hospital due to respiratory distress, at about six months old.

Left: In traditional isiZulu attire for Heritage Day (a South African holiday).

Above: Family picture taken for my grandmother's funeral programme; (from left) me, my cousins Liyema and Kungawo, my niece Sammy, and sisters Iviwe and Vuvu.

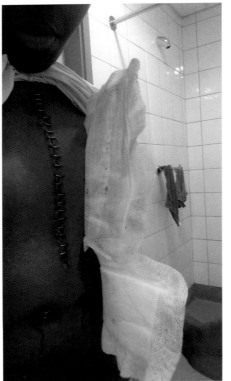

Left: The stapled incision after my second open-heart operation.

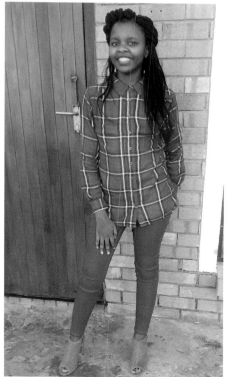

Above: Our group, Location Kids, performing at the Victoria and Alfred Amphitheatre, Cape Town. I am standing fourth from the right.

Left: Recovering at the Willows Resort. This is two days following my discharge from Provincial Hospital after my first operation.

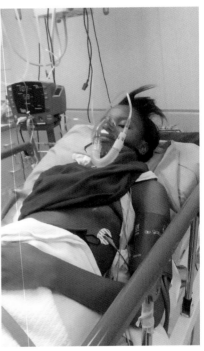

Above: On my way to the X-ray department on the eve of my second operation with my niece Sammy and her friend, Linathi.

Above right: Admitted to the Emergency Room, unable to breathe on my own before an operation.

Left: My grandmother holding Sammy after her christening.

Below: My grandmother, third from the left, with other sangomas.

Left: With my friend, Zolisiwe, on our way to our farewell at Abraham Levy Primary School. We rode in a limousine and had non-alcoholic 'bubbly' on the way.

Below: Chatting with my niece, Sammy, and her friend, Linathi, on my hospital bed, just before my second operation.

Above: Cruising in the bay on holiday in Cape Town. With (from left) Vuvu, Sammy and Lynn. This was after my second operation.

Left: My cheeky niece, Sammy, at age three.

My friend Zikhona and I after a fundraising walk at
Provincial Hospital. I often volunteer at the heart unit there.

Chapter 9

Township Life

Kwazakhele seemed to be growing increasingly dangerous. There was an atmosphere in the township. It is difficult to explain but it felt dark and threatening. We told Tony and Lynn, so, after about a year in Kwazakhele, they decided to move us back to our little house in New Brighton. They had the roof repaired and builders put in a concrete floor to replace the rotten wooden planks and then laminate flooring was laid down. The ceiling was taken down and a new one put in its place. Tony replaced the glass in the windows and we threw out our old furniture that had been destroyed by rats; we put in a new suite, table and chairs and a kitchen sink.

Tony's family in Port Elizabeth, gave us some really nice curtains and bedding. We repainted the whole house in new, fresh colours. Everything was clean and brand new; my mother would have loved what we did to her little house. So, we finally moved home to Singaphi Street, where my story had first begun.

The Red Location in New Brighton does not feel the same as Kwazakhele. In fact, every township is different. My grandmother loved Kwazakhele, and when we left she stayed there with my aunt and two of my uncles.

People try hard not to leave their homes after dark, for fear of being mugged or raped. Some girls are taken from the streets and forced into prostitution. Modern-day trafficking and slavery are still common events.

One day, my mother was walking home in the dark after working late. She was stopped and robbed by four men. They took her watch, earrings and cellphone. She was even more frightened and terrified to walk home alone in the dark after that. She even talked those men into escorting her the rest of the way until she was close to home. Better the company of these criminals who had not hurt her, than vicious drug-fuelled criminals who might have raped, injured or killed her.

My grandmother finally gave up on Kwazakhele after a disabled man was beaten and gang-raped in her back garden. His screams haunted her, and she moved to be with us in New Brighton.

Most township people are good. They are church-going and care for their families. They try hard to keep a nice, clean home. But there is very little work, which means no money. You can see and feel the desperation in many young people. They turn to drugs, gangs, and alcohol to escape; which leads to crime. A small number of criminals make the lives of our law-abiding communities miserable. However, many of us know hunger, true hunger, which is painful and makes you weak. I will be honest, if I had a child and my child was starving, I would steal for my baby; not for me but for my child.

There are other horrible crimes that happen. I have explained that there are good sangomas, like my grandmother, and some bad ones. Some sangomas have told men with HIV that if they have sex with a virgin child, they will be cured. So, desperate and sick men sometimes rape children and babies.

And recently there has been an increase in the kidnapping of young children. Most are never found, but sometimes they are found with parts of their bodies missing. These are called muthi killings. Muthi is traditional medicine. Criminal gangs kidnap children and remove body parts from their victims to sell to evil sangomas for medicine or witchcraft ceremonies. Some families, within metres of our home, have had children disappear, never to be found.

All of this – and more – will be familiar to my friends and readers from townships. For those from wealthy areas or living abroad, please know that this is just a very small part of the daily horrors of township life.

I once read that the average age people live to here in South Africa is 50 years. Tony says the average is over 80 years of age in the United Kingdom. It's not only violence that cuts lives short. We are also living with the worst HIV and AIDS epidemic in the world. All of this really saddens me.

I have seen too many people die as a result of HIV and AIDS. I am only an 18-year-old girl, but it seems simple to me. Boys – use a condom! Girls – insist that they do! Stay faithful to your partners. Get tested regularly. If you are having sex with people and you do not take precautions, nearly one in every five people could be infected. It is all around you, it is only a matter of time before you catch it, and it is killing us.

Condoms are free at the clinics. Use them and within a generation we could beat HIV and AIDS.

Chapter 10

The Beginning

When I was fifteen years old, my body was changing from that of a child in to a young woman. It was a difficult time and I really wanted my mother around. I had never bothered much with boys; I thought that they were arrogant and stupid. Some of my friends had boyfriends and for some reason, boys started to look more interesting, so I wanted one as well.

My friend Thami and I started to hunt for boys; we plotted and planned. I sent Facebook messages to boys to try and get them to meet up with me or date me. It was as if something inside me had changed and I did not know myself.

Tony found out. We had a conversation that I did not like and I was very uncomfortable. He has three daughters and three granddaughters in England, so he was used to chats like this. But as for me, a girl who even found it difficult to talk to her sister, I was so embarrassed. At first Tony was angry with me. He said that I lacked self-respect and I was not acting with dignity.

Then we talked properly. He was disappointed, but then he explained what was happening to me, how hormones would affect the way I felt. He asked what I would do if I chased boys and I actually caught one. I told him, 'I don't know.' But as I turned away, I said in isiXhosa, under my breath, 'But I will think of something.'

My changing body was the start of my problems. The arthritis had been under control but it started to give me a lot of pain again. I was growing fast and I would lose a lot of blood during my periods, which often lasted for many days at a time. Sometimes I felt weak and I could not catch my breath.

The first place to go when you are sick in the township is the clinic, where a nurse will see you. You have to go early as there are long queues of sick people. Sometimes the clinic has no medicine at all. They do give out a lot of paracetamol and calamine lotion, though. This is not much help for more serious problems.

In 2016, we attended a ceremony at home for Gogo. Our elders have a service to talk to the ancestors, to prepare themselves before they actually die. My uncle slaughtered a goat, which was cooked in a huge pot outside. I felt very ill after eating the meat and vomited. The nausea was very bad. Gogo made me chicken soup, but I was tired and sick and just went to bed. In the evening, I woke up, and people were still eating and drinking. The guests started to leave at around 9pm and we all retired to bed at about 11pm. At 3am, I woke up unable to breathe properly, gasping for every breath. I did not want to worry Gogo, so I woke my aunt and Vuvu, who took me outside for fresh air. I felt a bit better and went back to bed. I woke three hours later at 6am, again gasping for air; frightened and weak.

This was the beginning.

Chapter 11

Thank God for Dr Brown

I must have looked really ill and distressed because my aunt immediately called for an ambulance. In the ambulance, they checked my blood sugar levels – for diabetes – which were all fine. The ambulance took me to the Accident and Emergency Department at Dora Nginza, which we often call casualty. I was put on a drip to hydrate me. They told my aunt that I was pale and very weak. I was put to bed to rest. Blood samples and urine samples were taken, along with an X-ray of my chest. The doctor explained to me that the blood test showed that the iron in my blood was low; I was anaemic and needed blood. My blood group, AB, is rare, but they managed to find some blood and it was given to me via a drip in my arm.

I am sure that the doctor believed the cause of the anaemia was that I was bleeding heavily during menstruation. My uncle, aunt and sister were kind and took turns to sit with me. At first I had no appetite, but as the drips and blood entered my body, I started to feel better. My grandmother cooked some really good food for me and sent it to the hospital. I was annoyed with myself for causing so much trouble.

The following day, I was admitted to the ward. This had never happened to me before and it frightened me because many of the people I knew had died in hospitals. I tried to be brave and made silly jokes. On the ward, there were two free beds and the nurse asked me to choose one. I chose the bed next to a lady who did not look sick at all; I did not want to sleep next to sick people. Hospital rules meant that my aunt was not allowed to stay with me that night; my first night sleeping alone in a ward full of strangers. I prayed through the night, asking my mother to guard me while I slept. At 5am I was woken up by the nurses to bath, after which I had breakfast at 9am. This routine was one which became familiar to me. I remained in Dora Nginza for six days, most of the time feeling ill, nauseous and weak. I could barely get out of bed to go to the toilet.

Just before Christmas, even though I was still feeling very poorly, I was discharged from hospital and allowed to go home. It was Christmas Eve and Tony had arranged for lots of food and a large joint of pork to be delivered as a Christmas gift to my family. Before he left on his last visit, he had bought Christmas clothes for us, Iviwe, and our cousin Liyema. Gogo bought new shoes for the little ones. I had a wonderful, happy Christmas with my family.

A few days later, on 30 December 2013, I was sitting with my family when I started to hallucinate. I did not recognise my own family and they said that I was talking gibberish and seeing things that were not even there. I must have frightened

45

them; they thought that I was losing my mind, going crazy – or at least crazier than usual. They called an ambulance.

At Dora Nginza Hospital, I waited for nine hours to be seen by a doctor. I was then given an injection and put to bed. The doctor said that my brain had been starved of oxygen. I was given oxygen and aspirin, then discharged and sent home the next day. It was obvious – even to me – that something was wrong, and that I was not going to be cured by an aspirin. However, I was very pleased to be going home for New Year.

We had told Tony all our news and I knew that he planned to fly over as soon as he could to be with me. As we approached our home in the taxi from Dora Nginza Hospital, we saw Tony near his car, chatting to our neighbour. I was so pleased to see him. He hugged me and Vuvu and took us out for a huge meal to celebrate New Year. His arrival just then was a complete surprise.

Tony took me to a private clinic. My blood pressure was so low that the machines could not read it. My iron (haemoglobin reading) was also low and I was very thin. The nurses told me that they were surprised that I could even stand up!

We bought iron tablets as the nurse advised and Tony took me, Vuvu and Sammy to the Willows. He put a mattress, pillows and a duvet in the living room and opened the doors over-looking the ocean, to get my lungs full of oxygen. He did not want me to sleep in the same room as Vuvu and Sammy who would be using up the oxygen. He made me eat steak from the braai with salad and vegetables. That was not easy for me but I managed to eat it all. I slowly improved but I could not walk very far.

Over the next few months, I was getting sicker. I did not manage to go to school much. I was admitted to Dora Nginza or Livingstone Hospital on several occasions. I did try to get into school whenever I could, but it became tougher and tougher.

The doctors were not sure what was really wrong with me, but slowly they realised that there was a problem with my heart. They told me that I had the heart of a very old person; another said that it was pericardial effusion which means that my heart is surrounded by water. Then another doctor told me that my heart was twice the size it should be and that I had tachycardia – a fast pulse and heart rate – then arrhythmia, which is when the heart beats at an abnormal rhythm. Next I was informed that I had congestive heart failure, which just means that my heart did not pump blood like it should. After that it was problems with my mitral valve, a valve in my heart. I stopped being frightened and as I often do, I got angry. I realised they had no clue what was wrong with me. I had test after test after test done, and they could not work out what was actually causing the heart problems.

When I got angry, I was determined to beat whatever this was. To fight in every way that I could. Even if I was weak and frightened, I would never quit. I am not a quitter.

I was still getting thinner and weaker when I was referred

to Dr Brown and his team at Provincial Hospital. Thank God for Dr Brown. He was due to retire soon and was a very well respected and talented cardiologist. He immediately knew that there was something seriously wrong and he sent me for lots of tests, some of them in different hospitals. I had scans and X-rays, as well as many blood tests, until he began to get a full picture of my condition.

Finally, he diagnosed me with Left Ventricular Non-Compaction (LVNC), which is very rare. What it means is that a chamber in my heart (the left ventricle) had not developed properly. Instead of being smooth, the wall of my heart was weak and had ridges and recesses. The condition is congenital, but to this day we do not know who I inherited this from as many of my relatives are dead. We may never know. Dr Brown also said that my mitral valve was in a bad condition and might need to be replaced. As a child my heart had worked well, but as I grew older, the extra work required to pump blood around the fast-growing body of a young teenager was just too much for it.

I have asked Tony to write the next chapter. He spoke to my doctors and was there for me while I was unconscious or asleep, and he can tell you anything that I may have forgotten, or my where my memory is hazy.

CHAPTER 12

Surgery

Vovo had many tests before her operation, even spending six hours in a Magnetic Resonance Imaging (MRI) scanner at Livingstone Hospital. She was prodded and poked and had constant blood tests. Vovo always had a smile and never complained; she made jokes and kept all our spirits up. This, of course, was the wrong way around as we were all so worried about her. We were trying so hard to keep on a brave face through everything. She always remained calm and I believed in Vovo's quiet strength and positivity. The doctors and nurses all, by comparison, seemed a little gloomy, but Vovo told me many times, 'Tony, I *will* beat this!'

Dr Brown told us that he had never seen a case like Vovo's in over 40 years in practice. In fact, no one he knew had. When I asked for a prognosis and what his clinical plan was, he told me that there was no precedent set for Vovo's condition, and so it would depend on what the surgeons discovered when they opened her up. For the time being, they were just responding to her current symptoms.

It was a truly scary time. We appreciated how serious Vovo's condition was and we knew there was the real possibility of losing her, but we had run out of options and had to trust the team who were caring for her.

The night before Vovo's operation, the surgeon, Dr Gerhard Oosthuysen, visited her to explain the procedure and warn Vovo that all surgical procedures could be very dangerous, but this surgery would be exceptionally challenging and difficult. He explained that she would be put onto a bypass machine that would pump blood around her brain and body so that they could stop her heart. There was a danger that she could have a stroke or heart attack, resulting in death. Although this was very frightening for all of us, she remained calm and certain of her survival.

The operation was performed on the Fourth of July, which is Independence Day in America, and this was significant as we hoped that day would result in being *her* 'Independence Day'. We all prayed for her.

The surgeons made a large incision and laid open Vovo's chest. They already knew that her mitral valve was faulty, but what they also found was a huge aneurysm attached to the left ventricle of her heart. The aneurysm, they thought, could have been caused by the inherited genetic condition in her heart, causing the already weakened wall of the heart to balloon and fill with blood, which then continued to stretch and stretch, causing the heart wall to get thinner and thinner. This meant that it could burst, which would have resulted in instant death.

Of course the surgeons had expected some sort of fluid, because it had shown on all her scans that her heart was enlarged and appeared surrounded by it. The worst of all the possible outcomes would be blood clots forming in the aneurysm and breaking away and then travelling to her other major organs such as her lungs or brain. This would have had the same result, death. It would be a massive task and a huge risk for both Vovo and the brave surgeons, who had decided to take a chance in removing this huge bubble of blood and heart tissue.

The surgeons, with great skill, removed the aneurysm and patched the missing part of her heart. They then replaced the mitral valve. Finally, after six long hours, they closed her chest and sent her down to the Intensive Care Unit (ICU). The next 24 hours were long but crucial, in case of post-operative complications, which could have also resulted in her losing this fight for her life.

When I first saw Vovo in the ICU ward she was in a bed surrounded by silent machines, with tubes sticking out of her, keeping her alive. She looked frail and small, almost too fragile to touch. I held her hand firmly to reassure her and tried to force some strength into those tiny fingers. I was worried and frightened, but deeply proud of this wonderfully brave girl.

Later that day when I visited, I wasn't expecting her to be awake, let alone able to talk to me. She said that she remembered someone holding her hand, but did not know it was me. She did not remember me speaking to her either. Never once did

51

I doubt that my brave warrior would pull through this traumatic time, but this is Vovo.

Vovo was kept sedated, although her heart stopped several times and she had to be resuscitated. For this reason, the doctors fitted an external pacemaker to help keep her heart beating at a steady rhythm, and which would also help to restart her heart if it stopped again. At this time, her surgeons were still worried and even contemplated a further operation to install a permanent pacemaker next to her heart, but they decided to wait, as they didn't feel that it would be appropriate at the time. She was so weak and fragile and it would not have been in her best interest just yet.

The next day I met with Dr Brown, who was instrumental in Vovo's operation and care. I was accompanied by Vuvu and some members of their family. We met to discuss Vovo, her operation and the outcome. Dr Brown was frank, explaining that Vovo was an extremely sick girl; many people did not survive long with her type of heart disease. He said that she would remain not days or weeks, but months, in hospital. Dr Brown continued to say that it was difficult to say anything more as they were in unknown territory. It was a first for the whole team. We were all frightened for Vovo. I returned to the ward, and pushing aside the tubes, I hugged her as best as I could without hurting her. I could see that she was in pain, but she smiled up at me. I took her hand in mine, she looked at me with her big, beautiful eyes and said, 'They are wrong, Tony. I will be out of here in two weeks. I am a "die hard". Trust her to say that! I smiled at her, but I remembered the words spoken by her cardiologist a few minutes earlier. I did not doubt her wonderful courage, strength and resilience, but would it be enough? However, I was sure that if anyone could survive this, my tough little Miracle Girl could do it.

The surgeon visited Vovo in ICU. He was very pleased with her, saying she was a very strong person and that she was lucky to have survived. That strength and luck would be tested again, sooner than any of us could have dreamt possible.

Vovo badgered and cajoled the doctors to let her out of ICU and back to the wards. She is an irresistible force when she sets her mind to it. As her heart was working better than anyone could have imagined, with no further operation required, within a couple of days the nurses disconnected the machines, monitors and tubes that had kept her alive. She got up after five days and walked to the showers. Later that day she was transferred back to the wards.

It wasn't long before this amazing girl was harassing the doctors, once again, to be discharged. Now that Vovo was out of danger, I reluctantly returned home to the UK. It was a surprise to everyone except Vovo when she was discharged from hospital not months or weeks after major heart surgery, but days. Ten days to be precise and yes, she had amazingly achieved her own 'Independence Day'. She, of course, wasted no time in reminding me that she had told me that the doctors were wrong and that she was a 'die hard'.

Chapter 13

Ghosts, Ghouls and Other Spooky Things

In 2016, my grandmother started becoming ill and I was very concerned for her. She was diagnosed with diabetes. Gogo was a big woman who smoked a small isiXhosa pipe. She loved sugar, like most people, – five big spoons in her tea or coffee and she would also eat cakes and biscuits whenever she could get them. She knew that this was bad was for her, but she would not cut down. We tried hard to talk to her about it, but she would get angry. Angry is not the right word; she was more like a volcano exploding. We were worried because we could not afford to lose her as well, we really needed her. Occasionally, she was admitted into hospital. They adjusted her medication and made her eat properly. Then they sent her home again. She could not wait to get home for a big mug of hot, sweet tea!

After my operation in July of 2017, I returned to school as soon as I could. I had missed my friends and I wanted to catch up on my schoolwork so I could progress to Grade 12 and matriculation; that way we could all celebrate our farewell together.

School was great and I was doing well. I was not allowed

to do physical training or netball, but I was fine with everything else. I took 11 tablets each day. Some were diuretics used to flush out excess water from my body. This was tough because I needed to pee all the time, and some teachers would not permit me to leave the classroom. Often, I would sit with my legs crossed tight, then run from class to the toilet at the end of the lesson. Gogo was in and out of hospital because of her diabetes, which was so difficult for my family, with both of us, at times, in different hospitals.

Then, in September 2017, my gums started to bleed; I had to keep spitting out blood, my mouth just kept filling up. I went straight to Provincial Hospital, where, by now, I knew the doctors and nurses very well. I was immediately admitted for tests and observations.

That night, I woke as I felt someone's hands around my throat, and it was hard to move or shout for help. The nurses came and said that there was no one there and I was overreacting. I was scared because sometimes I see things, like figures that no one else can see. The nurses, and even Tony, say that maybe it is my medication making me hallucinate, or stress; just my mind playing tricks. But one night, I was sharing a room with six people and we chatted and became friendly. That night, I felt those hands around my throat again and I heard people whispering. I wanted to run and tell the nurses, but had second thoughts and just pulled the duvet over my head and kept absolutely still. At 5am, the nurses came into the ward to wake us and I told my ward mates about my bad night. Three of them said they had the exact same experience. We agreed to tell the nurses our story. So we showered and then we sat with the nurses. After we told them our story, they said that they could not say we were lying because other patients, admitted to the ward before us, had said that they had the same experience. Those nurses told us horrible stories of people who had died in agony in that ward over the years. I think my eyes were huge and the horror showed on my face, as they told the stories because they laughed. I told them I wouldn't sleep in that ward again; I would stay up all night. They added sleeping tablets to my evening medication.

I think that there are ghosts in hospitals where people have suffered and died, sometimes in agony. But you be the judge, was it medication and stress that made me see ghosts in that old hospital, or were they real? A week later I was discharged, and I was so glad, but I felt sorry for the new friends I left behind in that spooky ward.

Chapter 14

House Invasion

Returning home was always a relief and a happy time for me. I loved and missed my weird, wonderful and eccentric niece, three-year-old Sammy. Unfortunately, Gogo was in hospital again, but hopefully she would soon be back for hot, sweet tea and chocolate biscuits.

One very windy Monday night, my uncle was out for the evening and it was very dark outside. I needed to sleep because I had school the next morning, but I was awake because my instincts told me that something was not right. Around midnight, I heard sounds outside the window, like scratching. Everyone else in the house was asleep. I got up to see what was happening and there was a man trying to force open our window! I woke up Vuvu and she saw him too!

We called the police and my uncle and then we called the neighbours to warn them. My uncle and the police arrived at the same time; they checked the yard and surrounding area, but had no luck. The man was gone. We chatted for a while about who this guy might be and his reason for trying to get into our house, then we went back to bed.

Later that night, three men returned, forced the window open and broke into the house. We were terrified. They had a gun and a knife. They stole clothes and a Playstation console, which Tony had given to me. We gave them the little money we had in the house. When they heard police sirens, they said that they would be back and ran away. It probably lasted three or four minutes, but it seemed like hours. We held Sammy, Iviwe and Liyema tightly; they were screaming and crying. Worse still, we knew the main thug who had entered our home; he lived in the next street.

The next morning we went to the police station and gave a statement; we were given a case number. What good is a case number? The man we had identified was still on the streets days later.

We complained to the police, but they said that my sister and I must identify him in his home and where he drinks with his friends. We thought, *Is this for real?* If we were seen as mpimpis, we would become targets for every thug and criminal gang in New Brighton. We would be killed before we could be called to give evidence. The police knew this, and we knew this. The police do not care at all about people in the township. They think that we are all the same and deserve each other. They are like care-takers in a zoo, looking into cages, not caring if the animals hurt each other. I was so angry.

So we took our problems to the community and there was a meeting. We found out that this gang was terrorising many of our neighbours and that they had raped and robbed a lot of people. The outcome of that meeting? We should all get whistles. I am not lying to you – whistles. Oh my good God! Blow on your whistle while you are being attacked?! Angry? No, I was furious. My community has lost the courage and bravery it once had and was known for amongst townships in South Africa. I had hoped that we would come together, as we had done in the past, and warn these thugs that, 'If you attack one of us, you have attacked all of us'. I had hoped that we would go together, as a community, to the police station and demand that they take action.

The thugs were telling everyone around us that it was not over. They knew that we had gone to the police and attended a community meeting within minutes of it happening.

One dark night, a few days later, those three men broke into our house again by coming in through the roof. It is terrifying to feel so powerless in your own home. They searched for anything valuable; throwing our stuff around and shouting at us. One of the men threatened to rape my little sister, Iviwe, and our cousin Liya (aged seven and twelve). As he went to grab Iviwe, my aunt grabbed a kitchen knife and stabbed him in his back, as hard as she could. Once again, the police sirens in the distance caused them to unlock the door and run. The police must have passed them on the way, as they arrived only minutes later. They could not even catch the wounded guy, who moved slowly, leaving a trail of blood. Maybe I should have blown a whistle; that would surely have frightened them away.

Over the next few days, my uncle managed to borrow some money from his friends, and Tony sent money from the UK. We had burglar bars installed on our windows and a metal gate fitted over our front door to reinforce it. The workmen also put razor wire in the roof space. Sometimes, I hoped that they would break in again through the roof and while there, cut themselves to pieces.

One day, Vuvu went to the spaza shop near our house. Spaza shops are not like most shops, you cannot walk in and browse. The door is very securely locked. You walk to a little grill, like you would in a bank, and then you ask for what you want. They then take your money and give you whatever items you asked for. Standing next to Vuvu was the number one neighbourhood thug. She said that there was hatred in his face when he told her, 'This is not over. I am going to kill you!' She said that he meant every word and she was terrified.

But it was over. A bigger and tougher gang took them on. Number one thug was beaten near to death and ended up in ICU at Dora Nginza Hospital. He was badly beaten, his legs and hips were broken. He spent months in hospital and the gang told him that the next time he hurt anyone in Singaphi, he would die.

Chapter 15

Death of a Sangoma

My grandmother was very special to me. She had always played a major role in my life and I loved her so much. She was special to a lot of people in our family and also outside our family and neighbourhood. Many people saw her as a wise and powerful sangoma, and even though she had retired, people still came to her for help and advice.

I am certain that she knew her passing was near. As I mentioned before, she had insisted on performing the ceremony for her to greet the ancestors, which older people do when they feel they are on their way to joining those ancestors in death. She also carried out a ceremony called ntlamba peki. This is a cleansing ceremony for sangomas. Sangomas wear special beads that are handed down from generation to generation. This ceremony is a symbolic cleansing.

My grandmother was discharged from hospital on 4 August 2017. I had been home from Provincial Hospital for three weeks. We struggled to find transport to fetch Gogo from Dora Nginza Hospital, but eventually my cousin's husband offered to fetch her. It was 9:30pm before we finally got her home. What I saw was distressing. My grandmother was struggling to breathe, and she looked at us like she did not know us or even know where she was. It hurt when I realised that they had sent her home to die. Gogo was gently put to bed. She could not eat properly and we had to feed her using a tube. We didn't have the right equipment, so we had to buy it. My family and I gathered round Gogo's bed and we prayed for her. The others closed their eyes while they prayed, but I could not take my eyes off Gogo as she was struggling to breathe. After a while, she seemed more peaceful, so we left her alone to rest. Around one hour later I went in to check on her. She was sleeping, but with her eyes open. I took a chair and sat beside her bed. I held her hand and talked to her. I talked to her about my operation, school, and traditional dance practice at Location Kids. I could not tell whether she could hear or understand me. Then I told her that I loved her and that I would not be alive but for her; she looked at me and squeezed my hand. I wept a little, then I sobbed as I told her that I did not want to lose her, she was the last of the important adults in my family; all my grandparents and parents had died. While she squeezed my hand, I kissed her on the forehead.

I just carried on talking about anything and everything that came into my head. At 1am, Vuvu came into the room and joined me in talking to Gogo. After some time, we left her to rest and joined the rest of the family in the living room. We decided to buy the feeding tube the next day and that we would save some money to buy and build a shower for Gogo.

I returned to Gogo's bedside and took hold of her hand, and told her what we had been talking about. Gogo had to fight for every breath; she squeezed my hand very tightly. Her hand let go of mine as she stopped fighting. She stopped breathing. Gogo had just died; aged 65.

I tried to shake her and called her name over and over, but she was gone. I was crying so hard my chest hurt. My family came into the bedroom and we wept together.

My family tried to comfort me; they were worried that I might damage my heart, but I could not stop crying. I had just lost the most important person left in my world. I blamed myself for all the stress I had given Gogo with my illness and operation. It seemed that every time I became ill and I was admitted to hospital, it made Gogo sick as well.

My aunt closed Gogo's eyes and mouth. We then called the undertakers, who arrived at 5am. I did not want them to take her away from me, but my family made me go to my room to rest. I must have been exhausted because I immediately fell asleep and only woke up again at 8am. By that time, the whole extended family was arriving to pay their respects and help to plan the funeral.

I had been absent from school for a couple of days and I had not done any of my homework. My teachers were angry with me, but I was in no mood to argue or tell them anything. It was hard to talk about my grandmother without bursting into tears. I knew that I had to do something, so I took the opportunity when a teacher, Miss Ximbi, approached me. I told her my story as I wept quietly. She told the rest of the staff and brought my classmates together to tell them my sad news. My school friends are very special; the whole class said that they would be at the funeral and asked me about the arrangements. Their support meant a lot to me. Before the funeral service, on 8 August 2017, there was a memorial service. My friends from school, along with all of my classmates, attended that service as well as Gogo's funeral on 12 August.

The funeral was huge and the church was packed. People arrived in coaches and minibuses. This was a very traumatic day for me, but I set my mind to be strong for Gogo so as to give her the best send-off I could, to celebrate her life and her passing. A part of me did not believe that Gogo was in that coffin, but I watched as she was laid to rest in the same grave as her husband, my late grandfather.

After the funeral, we returned to the house in Kwazakhele and served food to all those that had come back with us. Some left for home, while some stayed well into the night. My family came together and we promised each other love and support, just as Gogo would have wanted.

As is our custom, the following day we all got up at 6am to go to that place where we speak to our ancestors. We rinsed our mouths out with milk, as is tradition – we do not use toothpaste before speaking to our ancestors. We prayed to God and then asked our ancestors to help and support our grandmother, to welcome her and to look after her.

Back home, we had breakfast and cleaned out the whole house. After that, following custom, people were asked to take any of Gogo's clothes that they wanted.

After the death of such an important healer, there are three ceremonies which must be carried out. The first two are led by other sangomas, who stay in our house for this period. The first ceremony is called ukuchitha iintsimbi or 'to throw the beads'. During this ceremony, my grandmother's ceremonial beads and jewellery are given to other sangomas who need them. We make umqombothi and serve a traditional meal of samp and goat's meat.

The second ceremony is umgoduso, or 'going home'. Taking a loved one home is a happy celebration and like a party. Apart from umqombothi, we serve brandy and vodka, and slaughter a large cow. We also serve that with the goat's meat, samp and cabbage.

The last ceremony is a family ceremony but family friends and neighbours are also invited. This ceremony is called umbuyiso or 'returning home'. Again, we have to feed everyone, and this can cost a lot of money. In fact, many thousands of rands.

But not one member of our family would ever complain about that money. We did everything required of us by our culture to say goodbye to the grandmother we loved so much. We know that's what she would have wanted from us and she would have enjoyed every minute of it!

Chapter 16

Infection

After Gogo's funeral, I was not well. I felt that I did not want to live on, but I knew that Gogo would be so upset and angry with me for thinking like that, and that I had to pull myself together and survive for my sisters and my niece. I also did not want to waste my life. For my mother and grandmother, I wanted to live a good life and become successful.

As you know, Vuvu does not handle stress well and we had a lot of stress. In just two months, we had to deal with my open-heart surgery, two house invasions with murder and rape threats and the death of our grandmother. We were all feeling really down, but Vuvu was completely distraught. Also, Vuvu had been dating a boy without telling anyone. Our uncle had a son who he had not seen since he was a baby; the mother had moved away. The boy's maternal family visited us to discuss his initiation ceremony as he was one of my uncle's clan. Can you guess? Yes, Vuvu was dating our first cousin! This is not a common occurrence, but it happens. For example, a 22-year-old friend of mine found out in 2018 that she had unknowingly dated her own brother. He had two other sisters, making them all her half-siblings.

Tony was annoyed because Vuvu had used money he had given her for college to visit this guy. As always, he was angrier about the lies that had been told, than about the money. Tony also wanted to discuss the concept of boundaries with her because of her college commitments and her duty to Sammy. When all this came out, she ended things with our cousin. One night, I was so worried after everything that had happened, because Vuvu had locked herself in our bedroom. She felt that she was a big disappointment to everyone, so she swallowed what was left of Gogo's medicine, in a very serious attempt to commit suicide. Our uncle smashed down the door and we called for an ambulance. The doctors and nurses at the hospital thought that this time she would die.

After a night where her life was on a knife-edge, she pulled through. I was angry with her because I was fighting to stay alive, while she wanted to throw her life away.

I, too, began to suffer after Gogo's death. My gums started to bleed again; they were a mess. The blood was running down my throat and I was gagging on it. In October 2017, I was once again admitted to Provincial Hospital. I was freezing cold and shaking, even though it was summertime, with temperatures at nearly 30 degrees Celsius. The nurses wrapped me up in blankets and gave me hot tea. The doctors took blood from me for testing. They used this blood to make blood cultures to identify infections in my bloodstream. In the laboratory, the technicians found a serious infection. They also found an antibiotic that could destroy the infection in my blood. They had rushed the results through and, within four hours, I was on an intravenous drip containing an antibiotic called Cephalexin. This was the most painful drip that had ever been inserted into me, and it was administered every six hours for two weeks. The doctors tested my blood and sometimes thought that the medicine was working, but the infection in my bloodstream returned stronger than ever. They changed the antibiotics and increased the dosage. They gave me Gentamycin at 9am and Vancomycin twice each day, at 9am and 9pm. I was losing weight quickly from 60 kg to 38 kg, losing nearly half of my body weight in just six weeks. It was bad. I was starving all the time, despite the fact that I ate and ate. Pies, KFC, lots of noodles, hospital dinners, home-cooked food – you name it, I ate it. I never stopped eating but my body was just not absorbing the food properly. And throughout all that time that I lay in my hospital bed, that infection was winning, and killing me.

I will let Tony tell you what happened next.

Chapter 17

'Ndubela is Dead!'

It was six o'clock in the morning. A team of surgeons, led by Dr Oosthuysen, came together at Provincial Hospital in Port Elizabeth. They were about to begin a long and difficult operation on 17 year-old Vovo, in a final, desperate attempt to save her life.

Vovo had undergone serious and complicated heart surgery just a few months earlier, but she had to return to Provincial Hospital when complications set in. Her breathing was poor and the doctors, led by Dr Brown, found an infection in her blood stream which originated from her heart. It appeared that she had contracted it during the first operation.

Laboratory tests had shown that the infection would respond to intravenous antibiotics, but it didn't. The seat of the infection in her heart was so bad that it just kept pumping more and more bacteria into her bloodstream.

After eight weeks of treatment, Vovo was told that, without surgery, she had less than four weeks to live. The infection would kill her. Her surgeon told her that this surgical procedure would be the most difficult and dangerous that he had ever performed, but without it the infection would prove fatal.

Vovo was prepared for theatre by the nurses early that day, Tuesday, 12 December 2017, just four weeks before her eighteenth birthday. She was visited by the anaesthetist and lightly sedated. She was wheeled into the brightly lit operating theatre, then transferred to the table. There she was put to sleep under general anaesthetic.

The incision to open her chest cavity was over half a metre long. Her rib cage was pulled open. She was going to be put on a bypass machine again while her heart was stopped for surgery.

You will remember that during her previous operation, Vovo had a mitral valve replaced and part of her heart was removed to repair an aneurysm. This was patched from inside the heart during that operation. What the surgeons saw when they opened up her chest cavity for this operation, stunned and dismayed them.

The doctors believed that if the infection was just in the synthetic mitral valve, it would be possible to replace it, but if the infection was in the area of the repaired aneurysm, success was far less likely. Dr Brown had warned that one option would be to just stitch her back up if surgery was impossible and let nature take its course, which would mean death within days.

What the surgeons saw that day was that the mitral valve and the area of the repaired aneurysm were oozing with infection. Vovo had a large abscess in her heart. Not only that, but a huge blood clot had formed next to her heart, also full of bacterial infection. No one on the team could understand how she could possibly still be alive with such a massive infection, especially after all the surgery and trauma her poor heart had already undergone.

Although devastated to lose her, it did not come as a surprise when Vovo's heart stopped beating. They checked the machines; her breathing had ceased and her pupils were fixed and dilated. She was clinically dead.

It became apparent later that suddenly Vovo could hear but not see. She heard her doctor declare, 'Ndubela is dead!' She could hear the doctor telephone the mortuary for her body to be collected. She heard them inform her cardiologist and the nurses in the ward that she had died. In that moment she knew that she must move, breathe, something, *anything* to let them know 'I am not dead! I am alive!'

As they began to prepare her small body for transfer to the mortuary trolley, a doctor saw her take a shallow breath. Despite it being several minutes since Vovo had been pronounced dead, the whole team worked frantically to stabilise her and went on to continue with the surgery, and with every minute that passed, believed that she surely could not survive the next.

The surgeons worked tirelessly, for many hours, on her. They replaced her mitral valve, cleaned the infected area around the patched aneurysm and cleaned out the huge clot of infected blood. Then they could breathe more easily. Seven hours later, as they stitched and stapled her up, Sivosethu 'Vovo' Ndubela had again survived against all the odds.

The operation was on 12 December 2017. Just over one month later, on 20 January 2018, after spending Christmas, New Year's Day and her birthday in hospital, the doctors reported that the infection had been beaten; that Vovo would soon be discharged from hospital and that she could return to school. A few days later and she was back in school. This was just six weeks after her second major open-heart surgery and lying, presumed dead, on the operating table.

Chapter 18

Finale

I made it. I survived. I recovered. I wanted out of that hospital as soon as I was discharged from ICU. My heart was working slowly, but well, and I was putting on weight. However, the surgeons still had me on an intravenous drip pushing antibiotics into my bloodstream, to make certain that the infection was completely destroyed. Finally, after another ten days in that hospital bed, the doctors announced that the infection was gone. I had spent four months in Provincial Hospital.

I have no memory of this, but two days after my first operation, I am told I was visited by my cousin, Phumela Tsoko. Still drugged, I could not understand what my cousin was saying so I shouted at her, 'Stop mumbling, just shut up and go and get me some food!' Phumela brought me a burger and fries from the local Steers. The nurses stopped Phumela as she was giving me the food, saying that I wasn't allowed junk food so Phumela tried to take it away. Apparently I shouted at her, slapping her and snatching the food back like a crazy, starved animal. Phumela fled, crying. The next day the nurses told me how rude I had been to my cousin, so I apologised to her and the family.

After my second operation, poor Phumela again brought me food; chicken with salad. I remembered what I was told about her visit from the first operation. I could not resist the temptation to tease her. I shouted at her, hitting out and telling her I wanted KFC, not this 'rubbish' she had brought me. The shocked look of horror on her face, and the tears in her eyes made me feel sorry, but I could not help but laugh. I think Phumela will give up on visiting me.

I was soon back in school. I was disappointed to be repeating Grade 11 when most of my friends had progressed to Grade 12. I had missed a lot of lessons, but I was grateful to have my life back.

I take tablets that I will have to take for the rest of my life. I avoid strenuous exercise but already I can do a little bit of traditional dance. I am strong, I love my life and I can plan my future. I regularly return to Provincial Hospital for outpatient check-ups and when I am there, I visit the doctors and nurses who cared for me.

Tony and Lynn came with me to greet them, and to thank them for never giving up on me. The doctor just said that he was happy to see me so well and that I was one of only five people in the world diagnosed with this rare condition. He said that he gave a presentation on Left Ventricular Non-Compaction (LVNC) and my case to other doctors so that they could learn from what happened to me. Like Tony, many of the doctors and nurses had also started to call me 'Miracle Girl' or 'Miracle

Child'. Tony, Lynn and our good friend, Sandra, who lives in Cape Town, had appealed to everyone they knew to pray for me. In Australia, the United Kingdom and in South Africa, people prayed. I later found out that the staff at Willow Grove, where we stay with our guardians, had turned the laundry room into a chapel and brought in a pastor; they all said prayers for me throughout my operation. It makes me feel like crying, but with joy, that so many people cared so much for me, a little township girl.

I survived, but many did not. I had a friend called Thembisa who needed a heart operation to replace two valves. She had a good job and she was still receiving her salary from work. Thembisa would often order takeaway pizza or KFC. When Tony arrived, he included her when he ordered food for me. We became close and she went into theatre for her surgery on the same day, just before me. We planned to meet up in the ICU after our surgeries. I never saw her again. The nurses would not tell me for a while, but she died in the theatre that day. So many died that I stopped asking about the people I knew.

Tony and Lynn flew over in February 2018 and brought with them their grandson, Ethan, and his friend Russell. Ethan asked whether he could fly over to help support me in getting well. I was a little worried about meeting him again because the last time we had seen each other, we were children and my mother had just died. This time he was an adult. I need not have worried; he had grown into a handsome young man and he was always well-mannered. He treated me and my sister with respect. We were to fly with them to Cape Town for a holiday, to help with my recovery.

Vuvu, Sammy and I were going to meet Tony, Lynn and the boys at the Boardwalk in Summerstrand, which is the beachfront and waterfront part of Port Elizabeth. We jumped into a taxi at Fish Funerals, on a large roundabout not far from our home. Yes, Fish Funerals. I have no idea why anyone would want to bury a cod or a hake, but that is what it says on the door – Fish Funerals.

The taxi we got into had pulled out in front of other taxis, cutting them off so that the driver could get to the passengers first. Taxi drivers only make money if they fill their taxis. There was only one other passenger with us on our taxi. Then three other taxi drivers jumped into the taxi. The first two were punching and kicking our driver when the third driver pulled out a long knife. He started stabbing and slashing our driver with it, like a crazy person. They were in the front of the vehicle, so we moved to get out of the door as fast as we could. We were so frightened! Sammy was too frightened to cry. Vuvu held her close, trying to shield her from seeing this bloody attack!

I think that a good English word for this would be 'surreal'. It was as if it was happening in slow motion. The taxi drivers were shouting, but our driver did not shout back or defend himself. He just sat in his seat, looking at them. Our driver was murdered that day. We managed to get off the taxi, but we were in shock.

We ran to get another taxi. Can you imagine how we felt when the murderer got into the front seat of our new taxi, wiping blood off his knife?! He started his engine and drove off. 'Shocked' does not even begin to cover it. We huddled in the back until we arrived in the city centre to change taxis to get to Summerstrand.

When we arrived late, I could see that Tony was both angry and concerned, but when we told him our story, he sat us down and gave us drinks and food until we could relax a little. He and Lynn hugged us tight. He asked, 'Why is it always my Ndubela girls in the midst of any trouble?'

I just don't know!

Cape Town was wonderful, as always. Vuvu, Sammy and I were excited to spend time with our 'other' family again. I was recovering, slowly but surely, and back on my feet!

Afterword: Dear Reader

My publisher, Andrea Nattrass from Pan Macmillan, along with friends who read the draft manuscript for this book have asked me to write an update of my story, so that everyone knows that I am still alive and well, as the book goes for printing. I feel so good and grateful to be alive. Even my wonderful, talented and skilful surgeon, Dr Oosthuysen, has said that it is a miracle that my heart survived the shock of two extremely serious operations so close together, in the condition that it was in, but without the second operation, I would have died.

After my most recent operation, I occasionally felt sharp, stabbing pains in my heart. This was caused by my reaction to the warfarin, the medication that keeps my blood from clotting around the areas affected by my operations. It was a little frightening and I was re-admitted to hospital for a few days while the doctors adjusted my medication. When I came out of hospital I took eleven pills every day but now it is down to five tablets per day.

After my first operation my heart ticked loudly like a clock – like the crocodile in Peter Pan – caused, I think, by my mitral valve replacement. It certainly attracted attention; the tick of my heart announced my entrance into any room. This stopped after my second operation. I have also put on weight. I love to eat and maybe I have put on a few kilograms too many, but I am becoming more active and capable and will be careful to follow the doctor's advice on nutrition.

I had a very special eighteent birthday before I was discharged from hospital. My doctors had mentioned my case to the organisation Reach for a Dream. The Reach for a Dream Foundation fulfils the dreams of children facing life-threatening illnesses and Dr Botha had written a testimonial about me and sent it to them. They do great work and it shone a bright light during dark days. They said that my first wish, of arranging my marriage to Jaden Smith, was a tough one, but my wish for a laptop they could manage. We had a big birthday celebration in my hospital cubicle, where they presented me with a new laptop, which will be a great help with my schoolwork. Jaden will have to wait.

School has been tough. As I mentioned before, I had to repeat Grade 11 because I had spent nearly a year in and out of hospital. It has been difficult to get into the routine of studying again. It is important to me to work hard, as I would like to become a doctor. I already know a lot about hearts!

The trip to Cape Town with Tony, Lynn and the boys was a really great holiday break. Vuvu and Sammy came too. We flew over there before our guardians went home to England, and we then went home to Port Elizabeth and back to school. Cape Town is a beautiful city. We had meals at the Waterfront and took a boat ride out into the bay. We all stayed in a big, four-bedroom house in the suburbs of the city. It was really good to stay with my English family and I did not let them see, but I had tears in my eyes when they left.

Another piece of news is that I am taking driving lessons. Tony made sure that he was leaving the country before I started. He says that I am, 'terrorising the roads of Port Elizabeth, and severe warnings of my route should be advertised on radio and television'. Funny? I don't think so! However, I am so grateful to Tony's friend in the United States, Guy Browning, who sent me the money to learn to drive. This is unusual for young girls from my kind of background and I am so excited! I am the only student in my school who is learning to drive and I love driving. Thank you, Guy!

I try to give back to Livingstone hospital when I can. I support and volunteer on the hospital's heart awareness days. I volunteer as a counsellor. This happened because a 14 year-old girl was admitted to hospital after having had open-heart surgery. She felt so good that she stopped taking her medication. Her condition soon deteriorated and before I could meet with her, she died of a blood clot which had formed because she did not take her Warfarin. The doctors had thought that a chat with a former patient, close to her own age, might help her and I am sure that I could have helped her if I had talked to her soon after her operation. I am also arranging a big concert, with Location Kids, for the hospital, to raise money for equipment for the wonderful doctors and nurses on P1, the ward where I spent so many months.

I still seem to always be in the middle of incidents and trouble that would be funny if not so tragic. In April this year my sister and I went to the funeral of a family friend. We were standing around the open grave, praying and singing. As the body was being lowered into the ground, the earth around the large tombstone started to crumble, and the tombstone fell into the grave, smashing open the coffin of our recently deceased friend and leaving her body for all to see. Just another day in the life of a township girl!

If I have learned anything in my young life, it is to not give up, no matter how tough things get. Don't let anything beat you. Even in the bad times, stay positive and, if you can, remain cheerful. It is not easy, especially over months and years when you are weak, sick and cannot breathe. Giving in to feelings of hopelessness and despair is so simple and at times it is what you want to do, but you must fight. Once you give up, you are done, it's all over. I also learned that people care, they really care. As children from the townships we do not feel it until something like this happens. There is a lot of desperation in our daily lives. That people from across the world came together to pray for me, and sent me love and support on social media, was amazing and humbling. Thank you, all.

With all my love
Vovo
xxxx

Glossary

anaemia A condition in which a person's blood doesn't have enough healthy blood cells, usually due to a lack of iron.

aneurysm A condition in which the aorta (the largest blood vessel in the body) grows a bulge, like a bubble, or the walls of the aorta become weak.

braai South African name for a barbeque.

bypass machine Hospital equipment that is used during an operation in which a person's heart has to be stopped. The bypass machine is used to continue pumping blood throughout the person's body until their heart can start beating again.

cardiologist A doctor that specialises in treating heart conditions.

congenital When an illness begins from the time a person is born, or it is inherited from someone else in their family and could only show its symptoms when they are a bit older.

intravenous When medicine is given through a small pipe that is inserted into a person's veins. The equipment used for this is called an intravenous (IV) drip.

mealie-meal 'Mealies' is the South African term for corn or maize. Mealie-meal is a relatively coarse flour made of ground maize. It is used to make soft porridge or 'pap', a stiff porridge that is a staple in most black households.

mitral valve The mitral valve is a valve that lets blood flow from one chamber of the heart to another.

mpimpi From the isiZulu word impimpi. Someone who cannot be trusted to keep important information to themselves. Especially information that could lead to trouble with the police or other authorities.

magnetic resonance imaging (MRI) A medical scanner that takes pictures of the inside of a patient's body. Similar to an X-ray, but it shows more detail than just bones.

nebuliser A piece of hospital equipment that is placed over the nose and mouth for a patient to breathe in medication or oxygen.

Panado South African brand name for paracetamol.

prognosis Before a doctor knows for certain what illness a person might have, they use the information they have gathered to form a prognosis. A prognosis is a description of what the problem could possibly be, before a diagnosis can be given.

respiratory failure When your lungs cannot get enough oxygen, which your organs need. This could be caused by another illness or being in a situation in which you cannot get enough oxygen.

sangoma The isiZulu word for a traditional healer. They work using both divination and herbal remedies to help patients. A new sangoma is chosen by the ancestors and goes through a rigorous training process with an already established sangoma.

spaza shop Part of the informal economy, these are small shops found mostly in townships and rural areas. They are often part of the owner's yard, either in the garage or a small room built in the yard. Spaza shops usually stock small food items and items for everyday use, such as lightbulbs, batteries etc.

Savoy Theatre A well-known performance venue built in Port Elizabeth in the 1950s.

umqombothi A traditional beer made from maize, sorghum and yeast. It can be drunk recreationally but is most often prepared as part of an offering to the ancestors.